Vulnerable Voices Of My Heart

From the Sky & of the Earth

Divyani Rai

BookLeaf Publishing

India | USA | UK

Made with ❤ on the BookLeaf Publishing Platform
www.bookleafpub.in
www.bookleafpub.com

Dedication

I dedicate this book to my loving family- Mum, Dad, Grandma and Sister; for without them ,this heart wouldn't still be vulnerable and thriving today.

Preface

Poetry has recently been my way of conversing with the unseen—an alchemy of emotions, memories, and states of being that words alone struggle to contain. These verses are not merely written; they are felt, endured, and transmuted from the depths of my consciousness.

In this collection, you will find whispers of inner battles, the echo of longing, the weight of fear, and the paradoxes of love and detachment. My poetry does not seek to provide answers; rather, it invites you into the ambiguity of existence, where beauty and pain dance in intricate synchrony.

Each poem is a fragment of a larger journey, one that traverses realms of shadow and light, despair and transcendence, reality and illusion. Some were born out of solitude, others from the raw collision of souls. But all, in their own way, serve as portals to an inner world I continue to navigate.

This book is an invitation. Not just to read, but to feel, to step beyond the surface and explore the spaces between the words. For in those spaces, perhaps, we may recognize parts of ourselves we had long forgotten.

Let these poems meet you where you are. And may they, in their own way, hold a mirror to the shifting landscapes of your own heart.

Acknowledgements

This collection of 21 poems is more than just words on paper; it is a journey, one that has been shaped by love, longing, and the unseen forces that guide me.

I am deeply grateful to the divine inspiration that moves through me, allowing these verses to find their way into existence. To the unseen muses, the whispers of higher realms, and the sacred flow of creativity, I bow in gratitude.

To my family and friends who have held space for me, whether in silence or in words, thank you for believing in my path even when I doubted it myself. Your presence has been a steady light.

To all those who have come before me and paved the way for art to be a bridge to the eternal, my deepest reverence.

To every reader who finds a piece of themselves in these pages, thank you. Poetry is a conversation between souls, and I am honored to share this space with you.

Finally, to my own inner child, the dreamer, the seeker, and the voice within; this is for you. You are heard. You are seen. You are home.

1. No Room for Error

One error and you shall cease to exist.

What next?

Everything will be as is yet you would have disappeared.

But everything cannot be as is when I disappear.

That is your delusion.

Your tiny world shall cease to exist with that one error.

Everyone you know in it shall disappear.

Close your eyes for a moment now.

Everything disappears but something else appears.

That darkness that appears is precisely the portal through which you shall re-appear!

2. Beyond the Horizon

I've traversed the jagged terrains of my being.
The journey appeared oh so endless.
Yet here I am and there you are.
Looking into each other's eyes, knowing where the soul resides.
There is something more beyond the horizon.

The knowing was dwindling.
The effects of the drug was ascending.
Yet Here I am and there you are.
Hand in hand walking down the lane which leads to us.
There is something more beyond the Horizon.

Smooth glazed starry nights keep me awake.
I wonder if I am forgotten or will be remembered.
Yet here I am and there you are
Witnessing shooting stars on rocks we lie.
There is something more beyond the horizon.

The moments arrived for us to unite.

There is no reason for separation, oh no more.
Traversing jagged terrains, the journey appears to end.
Looking into each other's eyes we know we're meant for us.
Hand in hand walking down the lane we are here for us.

From this moment on: I have, I feel, I can, I love, I speak, I see, I know
There is always something more beyond the Horizon.

3. We Hear You Call

Forever indebted to those who came before us
A strange reverence holds our heart.

Bound by traditions given to us
We surrender to their force.

The realms we inhabit appear too farce
For in it lies our remorse.

Together we shall overcome
This strange perpetual bountiful moss.

Reveal what once was the norm
Long before we knew our now abode.

A strange cocoon envelops us
Knowing we are not yet far gone.

The realms we inhabit appear all too frail
Overcoming those shadows lying in trails.

The energy of this initiation we know is magnetic
Treading this path with a little ambiguity they say is prophetic.

Farther along we see all beings floundering
Departing from their veins they are wandering.

Yet in there they discover their true reality
Solely by surpassing this menacing duality.

4. Free

Certain memories are ecstasy.

The kind I get intoxicated with while dwelling.

From the exterior, I assure you I am assumably back to pavilion.

I believe they wish to comprehend the incomprehensible.

 With my posterior well supported my sit-bones are delighted.

 My gaze wonders around the space engulfing me.

I realize my absence serves as a powerful reminder of my presence.

 Currently, I am a curious kid!

 In absolute joy and wonder at the happenings within and around me.

I would not deny the massive confusion and loss of clarity in me;

 A reminder - being gloriously human is an unrelenting blessing!

So far, I realize I have painted my story in broad strokes.

The time is perhaps now approaching.

The details shall orient me to my story unravelling as is.

Writing that thought down makes me feel free.

The pendulum is now set to swinging.

Swinging on the spectrum of fear towards freedom.

True freedom! The kind you get intoxicated with while swinging.

5. Speaking into the Void

When I call out to you, you respond.
When I don't call out to you, you don't.
What is this strange conundrum?

I for one know not what lies in between our lines.
When we speak of all things big and small
One spot I hold onto for about the length of our talk.

Two hearts skip a beat for about the length of one life.
It is strange to see you follow my lead,
When in reality I know not where to lead.

Often, wandering in the narrow lanes of our connection
I wonder whether it is my consolation, our connection.
You barely call out to me, I hear you still.

When you do, I ensure I am still.
What lies beyond this now I dwell on.
For I have found a happy place in my own thoughts.

Hues of sunshine paint my soul
The colors of which you barely know.
I try hard to explain to you where our hues come from.

You distract yourself with the sound of your drums.
You appear tired post which you lie down.
I for one know it is time to lie down once and for all.

I make no attempt to wake you up.
The moon rises and the sky changes its color,
I deeply wonder if I could ever have my honor.

6. Odd-yssey

Why does it feel so odd
Why does it all appear so bland.
The world where I come from is not here.
You tell me the land I belong to is right here.
I refuse to believe you no more.
I refuse to accept my fate no more.
This hurricane inside me is rattling all that I am.
This hurricane inside me is bombarding all of who I am.
I am who they told me I was yet I am who I know I am.

This melody in me is all that is real.
This song emerging through me is what I find real.
The long turns of winding roads I've walked has brought
me here.
The love I held oh so dear was a lie I told myself.
I reminisce the times I was asleep; for in that dream all
you had was me.
What a sad philosophy to want someone who shut the
door on me.

The ride alone was cold and dark, the stranger alone was God.

The sun rays pierced my eyes open, the stranger escorted me out

I wanted to fall asleep for in that dream all I wanted was for you to be me.

These terrains we tread are anew yet the landscapes we view are of you

The breath I take wakes me up, I see you.

The heart is green and the sun yellow

That lady was in black, that kid in pink, I in green barefoot on the tile.

The bottle was red, the coat grey, that shirt was white I remembered the moon.

We played Pictionary, the glass broke.

I spoke of baking bread, I spoke of bearing a child.

I knew it was meant to be, for me to find me. I wasn't lost just forgotten.

Now I Remember!

 I remember why I am here. I remember what for.

 It still feels so odd.

 I am now relying on that strange feeling I find endearing.

This land and its people I have now made my own.

The land I come from I am anchoring here in the now.

I accept to rewrite my past spanning eons,
I accept to rewrite the stories I've held on for too long.
This whirling wind inside me has now subsided.
This whirling wind has now ignited.
I am indeed who you told me I am and yet I am who I know I am!

7. Love is the way

Fascinated by stories of deep unrequited love between lovers across centuries.

It feels almost surreal to be loving a forbidden lover.

Why are we forbidden anyway?

To maintain a presumed order?

An Order where lovers are separated to render the entire human species extinct.

For soon we might be.

Because there is no choice they say.

Let us venture into the rabbit hole of ancient wisdom.

There are enough lovers.

There are enough of us across the world, beyond multiple borders.

Together we can unearth what has gone wrong.

High walls and deep ditches preparing to love everyone unabashedly every day.

Yeah! Call me crazy! Call me sick.

But Love is the way to be.

Love is the way.

8. How could I know?

I wouldn't know how you could not possibly know.

I wouldn't know why you would not let yourself be known.

Those ships have sailed from where you arrived, those waters dry.

My little sanctuary has survived, even though I have not yet fully revived.

Let me come closer within these silos you have built.

Maybe our warmth together could build up some heat.

With a lot of narratives on healing, are we really broken indeed?

I often ask myself in the silence of the sea... who am I?

For not knowing oneself hurts deeper than the thirsty drinking the sea.

I come here before you with all that I bear down on my knees.

Hoping you'd forgive me for all of what has been.

I wouldn't know why you wouldn't hear me plead.

I wouldn't know why you couldn't possibly see me bleed.

Pull me towards you, I know not your needs.

Or perhaps maybe I don't exist in your reed.

Wading through these waters, I get a glimpse of what could possibly be.

Your indifference haunts me with each passing second.

Even though this realization of your purpose resides in my heart.

This yearning for union will mostly tear me apart,

I would rather live in pieces all over this giant ball of water than jump into the fire.

For perhaps in this breaking, I will finally be free,

Dissolving into this tide, no longer seeking to be seen.

9. What is Really Real?

Why does it have to be so real?

This world which isn't all that real!

Why does the dream I hold need to disappear?

When all I want for it is to re-appear!

Tonight the sleep I had woke me up

Today all I can think of is the sleep that woke me up!

Those colliding worlds and my being breathing in all.

Why does it have to be so real?

This searing pain I hold in my heart.

They say a grieving heart sees the world a little differently,

Oh! I agree for when I grieve the whole world disappears.

Why does it have to be so real?

The lonely roads we take to be near?

Why does those roads lead nowhere?

When so many of us are on it to go somewhere?

The lantern burns bright yet the corner remains dark.

Who resides in that corner? Those aware of their own
cracks?
Those colliding worlds and spaces torn, the heart of it
remains in awe!
Why does it have to be so real?
The aching joints that no longer serve, the call to rejoin
the force.
Oh, I agree for when the call comes,
 I am halfway through my dream to meditate through
this world.

Why does it have to be so real?
The blocks placed to block the sight of what truly
matters
Why does the womb grow to grow on you
When drowning in its waters render you new?
They know they're lost when the call they make meets
with silence
But if only they realised the compass lies wherein
they've always been silenced.
Those colliding worlds in a constant flow, they appear oh
so more!
Why does it have to be so real?
This tiny bleed oh every cycle that nears?
Causing a searing pain, oh so real!
To let you know you're one with Her!

Why does it have to be so real?

Those existing worlds we run in so wild?

Why do our worlds not collide?

Are we meant to forever run in parallel lines?

What are these colours on the wall maybe you'll ask

'oh! If only I could tell you what they mean to me?

But you've already told me you underthink

So maybe I'll never get to show you what's really real?

Our worlds might collide but I may not forever be here waiting for it.

For in the wait it is not just me, it is me and my entire crew longing in deep.

The wait has already been long, I shall now dissolve into oblivion for you,

But know in your heart deep down, I attempted to show you what's really real!

10. Our Contract

Seeking to be more I resist a connection.
For in my seeking lies an inherent truth.
I have come a long way knowing I'd be here.
But little did I know you too would be here.
Gasping for thin air, I wonder if you knew all along
For looking at me, you seem so sure.
I panic because I don't know why are you so sure.
The day turns into night and the milk turns golden.
The stars appear in the sky and the moon disappears.
The sound of the bed creaking wakes our neighbors up.
Do you realize we have been here before?
The echoes of your heart throbbing resound in my ears.
The veins pulsating in my wrists makes you nervous.
Dreams of voyages to lands afar.
I dream of a land with seashores.
You look into my eyes with grave fear for you know you
are near.
When I look down, you quickly look away for you
realize its now time.
The time has now arrived to walk our paths alone.

You sense dread in me, you turn away knowing it is written in our contract.

You suppress. I regress. Together we digress!

Is this our fate?

I know not why we are where we are.

I continue seeking you in all where I go.

Unable to find you, I recede inside my hole.

This hole has now become me and I it.

Together we shall conquer that which has been unconquerable.

You wonder what that could be as you look at me upside down.

Its only a matter of time till we move past us like we never were.

I sense dread in you, I turn away knowing it is written in our contract.

I thrive. You contrive. Together we maneuver!

This is our fate to be held on to forever.

11. A Cosmic Hymn

I can hear her hum.
You have a home.
I join her in the hum.
Till Queendom Come.
Till all of us can become One.
We truly are from here now.
Though we've come from stars afar.
It's in the pain we have transformed
In the fire of this all-encompassing now.
Length of these years stretch as we glide
This plane as we know will mostly survive.
The ruins shall be forever to hold;
Until we realize empathy is the gold.
Whose world do you know?
Which world do you want to know?
The Queendom you shall know.
The memories are now resurfacing.
These echoes that resound in my being.
The distance apart shall soon dissolve.
For in my home, I have found our true home.

12. No Response

I am writing to you with no words in sight from your
end.
Tonight isn't too cold for my spine to bend.

This ache I feel in my bones is long overdue.
But I am writing to you with a heart anew.

The Sky was our home. The land is our home.
The descent into the now was indeed a spectacle.

For what else could have had us baffled
The disorientation from the fall off the ladder?

I am writing to you without a knowing of why we
couldn't begin
Obscuring your greys isn't the path to our bridge.

Trust and faith is probably why we'd forever sail
Far off into the land where we'd probably meet.

You resembled to me what once was a merry-go-round.
You were there with me while the world spun around.

Frolicking inebriated in joy you'd ask me to dance
I'd join not knowing what I would become.

I am writing to you here since you're gone
You'd probably walk back in if maybe I keep the doors
unlocked.

This ride back to me is so insane
I'd rather have me here than you here and me gone.

13. For you to Be Here Now

I am tired of playing it small.
The rules of the play appear blur.
These puny humans have got it all wrong
The mind falters and falls.

The yearning inside is deep and abound.
Where I exist, I laugh and I howl.
The ride is oft frustrating
But the company oh so endearing.

Is this really how it is supposed to be?
Is this really how It is supposed to begin?
Crashing and flowing through the crevices in the walls
The tower I look up to falls.

The ground beneath rumbles and mumbles.
It feels my anxiety pulsating through my nerves.
I am tired of playing it small.
When all I want is for you to just be here now.

14. Diving in Deep

It has been a timeless ordeal.

Getting glimpses of the fringes of heaven.

It happened as it did.

Quiet yet loud.

Of broken glasses.

Strange nights under missiles we drove.

We dove in deep.

We hovered as we spoke.

Those who dare believe, see.

What is this strange sensation I feel?

Spreading across my canals I feel my being evolve.

Dreaming shadows and loud whispers revolve.

Why has this daylight brought me home?

I have embraced my wild as I know.

Every time we exchange words, I lie low.

Knowing your defences too well, I hold.

Back in my mind, I resign.

Does it now mean we're deceived within the design?

I want this moment in time.

Cryptic desires wrapped in sheets.

Hiding behind words, I very well see.

Why do your words briefly submit?

Getting glimpses of the heaven I barely breathe.

What does this journey mean?

Will it be a forever ordeal?

I feel like I belong where I haven't yet been.

Do you get that feeling in your bones or is it just me?

I wish I could stop.

It isn't how I imagined it to be.

In my heart I know I want to only begin.

It sounds like a lot but why do we even exist if not for this?

15. Bleeding Air

Sometimes I regret for the things that did not take place.
Sometimes I wonder for all the things that did.

Why do we spend our time in unwrapping this gift?
 Am I now surrendering?

This gift reveals to me what no longer is.
That which I have been is now engraved on my grave.

Why do we partake in this revolution?
Is it a choice we have already made?

I want a say in the council; my voice needs
representation.
But can you hear me when I cannot even hear myself?

I know not why this plane behaves so strange.
I know not why I am the one estranged

.

There is admiration in abundance coexisting in this realm;
Yet here I am celebrating my own death.

This reminder serves as a powerful potion of transformation.
For what has been lost shall be found and what dies shall be reborn.

Why am I so strange? Why is this world I live in to blame?
All I want is for this night to swell for in it I want to melt.

Sometimes I wish for us to have dinner at the table.
Sometimes I wish for us to have a normal conversation.

I know we already do but I want to see you too.
This nothingness is choking my vein; I am bleeding air.

I hold no malice in my heart yet I hope you had.
Because then at least I wouldn't be receiving this gift.

Solitary in my own silence I now wander.
This role I find myself in, I quiver in fear.

Had I asked for what I have received or was it too a gift?

I shall be this curious and enquire for I want the answers.

The days are stretching far beyond my mind can run.
This solace is what I hold close to my heart.

In there I can refuse to bow down.
In there I can assert my boundaries and reveal myself to you fully.

You refused to bind yourself to me;
Because all we agreed to was freedom for me.

So, now I do not wonder as much for its working in alignment.
I am yearning for freedom within this divine design!

16. Her

I accept what exists here now.

I begin to prepare for what's to come.

The downpour thickens.

I sip from my glass of pale olive-green fluid.

My fingers trace the back of my ear,

my right knee pressed firmly to the ground.

My left leg extends; a single unbroken line from head to toe.

Silence encapsulates my being.

Smothering, smooth silence.

I am safely lodged within it, and it within me.

I close my eyes. I see her.

I make an intention again; I see her.

She is there, always, watching, guiding.

I tune in to her rhythm.

My body moves past the green meadow's vastness.

The rainbow canopy propels me forward.

I roll down the hilly trail, a voice guiding me all along.

I listen. I trust.

The hill delivers me to the mouth of a cave.

I reach forward. Darkness breathes inside.
I glide forward, safe within the womb of the unknown.
There is only forward.
I embrace the dark, and with it; I begin to remember.
I see her again.
She stands before the far-off ocean, her back to me,
her white garment; dimensionless, boundless:
screaming freedom with every single movement.
The rocks around us breathe.
The dance of manifestation takes form as I stand still,
my feet planted, firm.
Clouds sculpted in thought dissipate.
The sky as is dissolves.

17. Not in Love

Watching my demons fly high
I watch you gradually contract.
This perishable moment engulfs our union.
What could possibly be in the face of this mighty adversity?

No fear can have its grip on me I believed.
Only to see you fearing me, I realize.
There is much more behind those water ridden eyes.
How could I have possibly known the arrival of this calamity?

I quiver in a corner unable to truly fathom the intricacies.
This palpitation cripples me and my imaginations disown me.
Why such brutality wearing a veil of mediocrity?
I shall now allow for me to only walk around in obscenity.

This heart I hold in my chest is forever mine to keep.

But the heart you hold in yours is one that probably gives in.

The conundrum encapsulates our being for in this imbalance we reside.

All said and done, at least we are not in love to say the least.

18. A Warrior of the Heart

I will always keep wondering what transpired in your being.
For you to have cut ties with my being!
Too afraid of pointed rejection, I receded into the abyss.
I'm a warrior at heart otherwise but I got to keep my ecosystem alive!

No, you do not get to walk through my door again.
For you abused the trust I forever gave.
Too naive was not my weakness, you see.
I'm a warrior at heart otherwise just with my armour down at times.

I mirrored you your pain, you could not bear.
I will forgive you for I already have in ways I never could.
There is no possible balm that would soothe my being.
I am a warrior at heart otherwise only to reveal my wounds at night.

Where's home I often wonder for when our hands met I knew I couldn't falter.
But now with your hands gone, I know I can alter.
Alter these visions I held onto since the moment we exchanged our vows.
I'm a warrior at heart otherwise with really just one bleeding heart!

I see you thrive in your world unbeknownst to the creations you triggered in mine.
I let you in my home in the mothership they sent for me.
One tiny step towards you and the entire tower collapsed.
I'm a warrior at heart otherwise only to realise I am born a warrior with an invisible tribe.

Stitching up my wounds I now know you were never here.
My demons are real. I no longer wish to let myself be unreal.
You were only probably a figment of my reimagined imagination.
I am however a true warrior of the heart with multiple stitches; running across this land now with no fear!

19. Calling in All Parts of Me Back Home

I dreamt I was sliding down a hill.
I dreamt I was being looked at from afar.
I wondered who could be looking at me.
Soon, I wake up for in my dream I go astray.
How could I be gone where I truly am from?
How could I be here if not from there at all?
This longing I have in my heart shines through it all.
Therein lies the choices we make to always be here.
I call in all parts of me back home.
For when we met, I was alive and whole!

I dreamt I was dancing by her shores.
I dreamt I was being carried on his shoulders down the road.
I wondered where I was headed.
Soon, I realize I wanted to be carried and not let down.
I held on too tight and for once I fell off.
How could you let me fall from where I truly am from?
How could I let go when all I held on to was for you?

These soundscapes I now immerse in truly aggravates
the me in me.
Therein lies those moments I have always found dear to
me.
I call in all parts of me back home.
For when we are meeting now, I am half hidden with
snow!

I dreamt I was being loved in her arms.
I dreamt I was running from everything and everyone
afar.
I wondered where could I head.
For then I remembered I owed my being to her.
I was being nurtured in her womb whilst she birthed me
in here.
How could I possibly render her bare?
How could I possibly want her have me go astray?
The escapes I have formed within shall always remind
me.
This dream I now live oh so gloriously has been here
before me.
I call in all parts of me back home.
For when we shall meet now, your grace would have
thawed my snow for me to be whole!

This dream I am living is not just mine.
I share it with my ongoing tribe.

They're flourishing in different corners of the globe.
I get to witness their journey through a port.
I for one feel like I am right where I began from.
But deep down I know my invisible journey is one to
applaud!

20. Where it All Began

I met a fellow co-traveler and fell in love.
As crazy as I was, I announced it to the whole wide world;
my world.... because I believed in the intensity of its authenticity.
That love exchange terminated under strange circumstance.
I let the reins loose.
I feel a sharp pine-needle like sensation.
 I begin to dive and dwell longer into the processes of the how's and whys'
That inability of the reciprocation of the felt love annoys my depths.
But sometimes you let yourself grieve
And trust that you won't grieve longer than the situation deserves.
 Now allowing myself to grieve because no matter its duration in earthly space -time continuum
The love experienced remains eternal and indestructible.
Its unceasing force may gather dust in books unread

And breaths held longer to mend aching hearts
 but the sanctuary of peace it helped create shall last for
years to come.
The call I believe in whatever seemingly difficult
situation is only for further expansion.
 I shall honor that call...always.
 I open my mind, expand my vision and receive the light
and love of my divine family.
 Now...so be it. And so, it is.

21. Mu Here

For times that have long gone by
For hearts that have remained intertwined.
The winding roads lead me home,
Tonight I call you home.

For times that have long gone by
The ache in my soul rejoices.
The winding roads lead me home,
Tonight you can call me home.

These words mean forever more than words could ever mean
Our love alights this land we tread for in our hearts we stay.
These words mean forever more than words could ever mean,
You seem so beautiful since the day we arrived.
It has been a long wait I must say.
For you to return to where I always was.
Yet little do you know, I travelled too.

And got back to where we began from.

Yes I've known you since forever, Yes I 've felt you always
No amount of pain or grief could ever keep us apart ever!
Our separation was simply an illusion
We've always been one since forever.

For times that have long gone by
Let us raise our glasses in joy
The uncertainties fade away.
Tonight we call each other home.

For times that are yet to arrive
I promise to honor you each day everyday
Our existence in togetherness
Shall create Mu right here.

www.ingramcontent.com/pod-product-compliance
Lightning Source LLC
LaVergne TN
LVHW021305200726
843509LV00012B/1789